Joy is . . .

365 KEYS TO LONGEVITY

Paul Abell, Ph.D.

Published by Best Seller Publishing®, Pasadena, CA
Best Seller Publishing® is a registered trademark
Printed in the United States of America.
ISBN: 9781790582754

This publication is designed to provide accurate and authoritative information with regard to the subject matter covered. It is sold with the understanding that the publisher is not engaged in rendering legal, accounting, or other professional advice. If legal advice or other expert assistance is required, the services of a competent professional should be sought. The opinions expressed by the authors in this book are not endorsed by Best Seller Publishing® and are the sole responsibility of the author rendering the opinion.

Most Best Seller Publishing® titles are available at special quantity discounts for bulk purchases for sales promotions, premiums, fundraising, and educational use. Special versions or book excerpts can also be created to fit specific needs.

For more information, please write:
Best Seller Publishing®
1346 Walnut Street, #205
Pasadena, CA 91106
or call 1(626) 765 9750
Toll Free: 1(844) 850-3500
Visit us online at: www.BestSellerPublishing.org

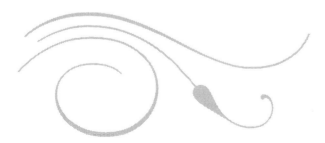

About the cover

On the front cover of this book, the author requested that the graphic designer include the Asian logographic "kanji" picture-writing character for the concept of *Longevity or Long-life*. On the back cover he included the logographic "kanji" character for *Joy*. Hopefully, the wisdom contained in the book will be your bridge for understanding the vital connection between these two essential concepts. It is only fitting that these logographic characters be included on the cover because much of the philosophy in the book regarding the true nature of joy that ultimately leads to longevity does stem from the traditional teachings and philosophies of the Asian cultures. Furthermore, as a practitioner of a form of Traditional Chinese Medicine, the author is deeply aware of the ancient correlations in the foundational philosophy of the Chinese Five Element theory. In that system, Joy is the balanced emotion associated with the Fire Element and the corresponding color is red. That Fire Element is symbolic of the energetic system regulating the heart and spirit. Within the complex interactions between all the elements and the organs that they represent, it is the Fire Element which truly dominates all the cycles of energy and, ultimately, the lasting vitality of the body. In other words, Fire-Joy-Spirit-Heart energy is the key to having health and length of years . . . the very theme of the book.

Dedication

I would like to dedicate this book to my darling wife, Liza and my precious son, Nolan. They are my ultimate joy in life and my inspiration for living until the year 2046.

Others to honor who have been a major influence in my life: Drs. Sidra and Hal Stone, Dr. Carolyn Conger, William Brugh Joy, M.D., Dr. Nora Weckler, Dr. Bruce Hector, David Spangler, J. Krishnamurti, Swamji Chinmayananda, Sri Aurobindo, Tibetan Lama Sogyal Rinpoche, Dr. Carl Jung, Ram Dass, Thich Nhat Hanh, Wayne Dyer, Kahlil Gibran, Joseph Campbell and the teachings of Lao Tsu, Buddha, and Jesus.

Perhaps the most formidable force shaping my consciousness has been the countless everyday encounters with my fellow travelers along the path of life. Each has been a karmic teacher of living truth in some manner, profound or incidental.

Commentaries

"Dr. Abell is a powerful and experienced healer, uniquely conscious of the complex secrets to longevity . . . one who is actually living the profound truths written into his new book."

–Hyla Cass, M.D.,- Internationally acclaimed health
expert and author of the book, 8 Weeks to Vibrant Health.

"Dr. Paul Abell's simple and timeless phrases are accurately tuned to the thoughts and questions that arise during the later years of life. This book provides a thought-provoking, yet comforting, companion for those entering the later stages of our life's journey."

–Drs. Sidra and Hal Stone
Creators of Voice Dialogue and authors of "Embracing Your Inner Critic"

"Dr. Abell is a genuine master of Holistic Healthcare. As a professional biochemist and scientist I have personally experienced the validity of his multi-level approach to attaining greater health, self-awareness and a long life. This succinct new book could well be the Longevity Tao Te Ching for our modern world."

–Dr. Donald F. Haggerty
retired academic career investigator in biochemistry and former Associate
Professor at the University of California at Los Angeles U.C.L.A.

"Dr. Abell has comprehensive knowledge about how the body works from both an Eastern and Western medical perspective. He is the Lee Strasberg of the alternative healthcare world . . . truly a master!"

–Anna Strasberg,
The Lee Strasberg Theatre and Film Institute

"Dr. Paul Abell is a consummate healer. He is skilled in the arts of wellness coaching, longevity training, Chinese Medicine and psychological process. He is well respected in the Los Angeles alternative health care community."

–Carolyn Conger, PhD - teacher and author,
"Through the Dark Forest: transforming your life in the face of death."

"Dr. Abell has amazing knowledge regarding longevity. He has an incredible talent, with healing powers and a unique understanding of the body. After so many years using his services, I have a well-rounded awareness of his deep, insightful sense of complete health and longevity. He has a special gift that he gives to all of his clients."

–Lyn Lear(Mrs. Norman Lear)

"I have known Dr. Abell's work for over thirty-five years. The wealth of simply-stated enlightened knowledge regarding health and longevity contained within his book is an extremely valuable blueprint for living a vital and fulfilling long life."

–Susan Winter Ward,
Author and Creator of "Yoga for the Young at Heart" programs for seniors.

"Dr. Paul Abell was a pioneer at the advent of the Holistic Health Revolution which began in the early 1970's. He has integrated the use of the Asian Healing Arts, Western Psychology, herbs, supplements, lifestyle counseling, multiple approaches to energy healing, and longevity principles from around the world. I honestly say he is a rare and unique authority when it comes to someone who knows the philosophical and psychological keys for understanding what is required to age gracefully."

–Jay Grossman, D.D.S. Clinical Assistant Professor at UCLA College of Dentistry and co-founder with Sharon Stone of the Homeless-Not-Toothless Foundation, a charity offering free dental care for the indigent.

"For over the 25 years I have seen the breadth and depth of Dr. Abell's work across many settings and many modalities. He brings a well-balanced understanding of Chinese Medicine, Energy Healing, Psychology, Western Science and Medicine as he applies them to his well integrated wellness theories and lifestyle consulting for those seeking longevity."

–Dr. Elena Bonn, Psychotherapist

"Dr. Abell's book, "Joy is . . . 365 Keys to Longevity," is a bit more sagacious and challenging than most readers might expect from the title. In truth, the book is a profoundly comprehensive collection of powerful health and lifestyle principles that provide a scaffolding for creating a fully-realized experience of living. If one would successfully internalize each of the consciousness concepts, life would indeed be filled with great joy."

–Michael Levine
CEO-Michael Levine Media

"As a respected elder in the consciousness community and through his own endeavors of absorbing the knowledge and teachings from many master teachers, Dr. Paul Abell has spent his life delving into the deeper mysteries of health and the essence of longevity. He is continually on the search for anything that will improve the quality and quantity of life. This book is a profound reflection of that journey."

–Lawrence Novick, PhD - Life Coach and Aikido Instructor

"My own healing path has been enriched from knowing Dr. Paul Abell for over 40 years. His unique approach to understanding the mind-body energetic connections transformed the healing skills of my advanced students at the Acupressure Institute in Berkeley, California. Paul's brilliance in teaching my students real-life lessons, blending the best of Western Somatic Psychology with the Chinese Five-Element Theory, offered healing practitioners advanced access to their own growth and their client's health and longevity."

–Michael Reed Gach, Ph.D.
Acupressure Online Programs

"Dr. Paul Abell's healing work and counseling has made a huge difference in my life. Paul has an impressive breadth of knowledge about health, healing, and psychology. His real forte is deep understanding of the relationship between lifestyle, emotions and physical imbalances. Perhaps equally important, he has the gifts of compassion and caring. He obviously loves what he does, and it shows!"

–Diana Ungerleider- Co-founder of the Fibar Corporation."

"As the senior Pilates instructor at my own Wellness Center in Beverly Hills, I mainly worked with Hollywood's top celebrities. Many of them had chronic structural problems which required more specialized physical care, often beyond the scope of traditional Western Medicine. Consequently, I referred those difficult cases to Dr. Abell to bring my struggling clients up to a level where I could work with them better. Dr. Paul not only helped everyone I referred, but he also got me through a very bad accident I had. His unorthodox approach to health care attends to the psychological aspects of physical disorders in the body. His technique accelerates the healing process and provides more lasting outcomes. Dr. Abell's years of experience in the Asian system of health care, combined with his own eclectic array of Western healing techniques and innate gifts of bringing the body back to into perfect balance, made him "the real deal" in an entertainment industry that requires quick results. He is an excellent example of a world-class mind-body health coach for those on the road to wellness and longevity.

–Siri Dharma Galliano
CEO-Live Art Pilates, Inc

"Dr. Abell knows what few people in the health care world know, because he has blended a lifetime of learning about the psycho-somatic cause of illness and physical disorders from many   healthcare viewpoints from cultures around the world. He has blended the most helpful aspects of those disciplines into his own unique approach to attaining wellness for his clients."

Emese Williams
76 year-old client of Dr. Abell and ardent believer

"Dr. Abell is living proof that the Longevity principles work. His wisdom, knowledge and passion will motivate you to live longer and feel better!"

–Jason Sands,
Vice President , Wells Fargo Bank

Dr. Paul Abell astutely transcribed his personal truths through the lens of one word, that feeling we all strive for in our lives, Joy! His new book is the synergy of philosophy, poetry, and wisdom from the around the world. It reads like a thoughtful meditation, easily accessible in its profoundness and simplicity. Dr Abell illuminates poignant ideas that are very crucial in our chaotic and distracted times.

–Shane Dultz, Ph.D.
Physicist and Medical Device Developer

The evolution of the book

When I was a younger man, while having a career in the Holistic Healthcare profession, I made a pact with a colleague of mine who is a Ph.D. in biochemistry, that we both would share our hundredth birthday together. My work at the Pritikin Longevity Center and my own private practice doing an esoteric healing art from Japan, known as "The Art of Longevity," certainly kept my focus on that topic alive. Through the years, as many, many birthdays sailed by, my scientist friend and I would often joke about the approaching possibility of sharing our 11th decade of life together. However, it wasn't until I fathered a child at age sixty-five, that my casual commitment to being a centenarian turned to a passionate quest. Both my wife and I had lost one of our parents as teenagers, as did my own mother before me. I vowed to not let that unfortunate legacy continue with my own son. Towards that end, I began an intense research into the science of longevity like never before.

In the nine months preceding the birth of my son, I read scores books on the topic of longevity and my library of health and wellness books that I had previously read exceeds four-hundred. Since I had majored at my master's degree level in college in Human-factors system engineering,

I took that system-analysis approach to the huge volume of information at hand. I created a Longer-life Matrix of the multitude of factors sited in the research that was, in some way, correlated to longevity. In many respects, I ended up even more frustrated and confused because there initially appeared to be mounds of data with no underlying G.U.T. (general unifying theory) for what fosters longevity.

In all of the research, much of the common traditional thought as to what allowed certain individuals to live longer was quite inconclusive and contradictory. As one might expect, genetics, a healthy, simple lifestyle and old-fashioned luck are major factors in living a long time, but other sociological factors appear to be even more critical. After working with the matrix for a couple years and stepping back with an overview perspective, it finally dawned on me that there *was* a common thread tying everything together. JOY of life was the single most prevalent emotion looming behind it all the factors in the matrix. But what is joy? The definition varies depending on what source you quote. Nobody seems to have a truly tangible explanation. Consequently, I began writing down brief summaries of every experience, personal relationship, peek adventure, profound quote, significant philosophical and psychological principles that related to the subject of that elusive elixir of life . . . joy.

When I reached almost two thousand entries on my list, one of my close friends suggested that I should publish it, IF for no other reason than the book would be a valuable autobiography and legacy of truth to

leave for my son. However, the sheer volume of information was just too massive for any one book. Another dear friend, a published author herself, suggested that I edit out the essence of truth and wisdom contained within my mega-manuscript into three-hundred and sixty-five salient and pithy one-line statements. The idea being that, by using such a format, an interested reader could do a meditation each day on what is the essential mindset and real-life behavioral lifestyle required to promote joy and the concomitant longevity. My friend's idea was a brilliant one.

The project became a monumental task of using Occam's razor to prune away anything that didn't succinctly state a fundamental principle related to joy and length of years. What remained is an anthology of treasured wisdom accumulated through seventy-two years of personal experience, intense study, research and related philosophy learned from many different academic and spiritual masters.

Many of the entries in this book are so very simple and self-evident, but powerful at their core. Some may seem cliché or pedantic at first glance, but to sit in contemplation of them can open unknown doors to deeper truths and create awareness for change known to be essential, but often ignored, for attaining longevity. Collectively, this book presents a blue-print for how one might live a practical, yet spiritually-aligned lifestyle that has the potential to facilitate living a long time. Of course, there are no guarantees, but in having the focus to manifest such a purposeful mindset one may possibly have a little better shot at having length of years.

Acknowledgment:

Some of the concepts and principles in this book have been learned from various spiritual, academic, metaphysical, and motivational teachers, gurus, and masters over many decades. Therefore, this writer would like to honor and credit those teachers for the foundational knowledge contained within this book. In truth, much of the content of the wisdom in the book has been passed down to those modern teachers from a lengthy legacy of ancient masters, now deceased. Consequently, parts of this book are, in a sense, an anthology of traditional philosophy for which no one person could ever claim ownership.

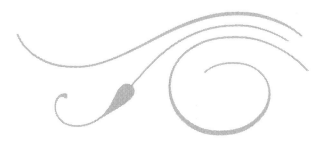

Introduction to the Joy is . . . Longevity Meditation

If you have gotten this far into this book, the odds are that you have more than a passing interest in living to a ripe old age. Be assured you are not alone! Since the dawn of civilization we mortals have been obsessed with finding the secrets to longevity and even immortality itself. Of course, as of yet. no known immortality potion has been found, but the search continues.

As mentioned in the "Evolution of the Book" section, I have come to believe that the quality of "Joy" is the elusive unifying characteristic most common to those who have length of years. In other words, the joy of living delineates those who are more likely to reach the ranks of the centenarians. The quantity of your years is directly related to the quality of your life. Of course, what creates joy is a wide spectrum of experiences that vary greatly between the sexes, and among ethnic groups, cultures, and nations.

In this work-book, I will be sharing my list of philosophical and practical concepts that may be helpful in finding and promoting true joy in your life. The content is the result of over seven decades of pursuing a

passionate interest in philosophy, psychology, religion and wellness. These pages hold the essence of what I've learned over those years regarding the keys to that elusive longevity-promoting state of consciousness known as joy. Some passages are simple and basic, some are more abstract; but all are in some way relevant to the quest for joy.

My suggestion would be for you to NOT read straight through the book. Rather, consider taking one page each day and actively contemplating the meaning of the passage contained therein. To do so, you might want to follow these few suggestions:

1. Do your meditative contemplation exercise early in the morning before the hustle and bustle of the day begins and while your mind is fresh.
2. Find a quiet place, away from all distractions, especially those of an electronic character. If you can find a place in nature, even if only a flower garden or special tree all the better.
3. Sit in a comfortable chair.
4. Start by closing your eyes and taking five long, deep breaths.
5. Open your eyes and read the sentence on the "page of the day" at least three times.
6. Close your eyes and think carefully about what is written.
7. Ask yourself these questions: Is the concept relevant to you? Is the idea something old or new for you? Would living the words require a new approach in your lifestyle? How might you apply the concept to the way you function that would bring more joy into your life?
8. If the passage speaks to you strongly, make an affirmation to include that awareness in your daily experience.

Of course, you will find a few entries that may not seem like they apply to you at first. Perhaps some concepts are totally alien to your way of thinking. Other statements may not even make sense at first glance. Whenever you encounter such pages, my recommendation would be for you to focus on those concepts especially hard. Those puzzling pages may be the most significant for you and relevant to you, because the best opportunity to expand your awareness often dwells within ideas that are unfamiliar, challenging, or disowned.

I hope this little compilation will give you reason to ponder and discover joy in your own life. Here, in these pages, you have potentially one full-year's worth of personal explorations. If even a fraction of the ideas speak to you at a deeper level, you might just add some extra days to your life or, at the very least, add a little more joy to whatever days you are blessed to live.

#1

Joy is . . .
having learned about
a practical key to longevity—
life-enhancing joy itself,
something potentially within our grasp.

#2

Joy is . . .
the rewarding sensation you get
whenever your love
is cherished by someone very special
who returns pure affection
back to you.

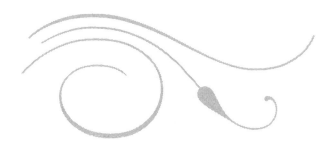

#3

Joy is . . .
understanding that our highest purpose
is to give love and service
to the planet.

#4

Joy is . . .
living grounded
in the present moment
from moment to moment.

#5

Joy is . . .
when your heart and soul
are filled each day
with the unwavering numinous love
of the infinite spirit.

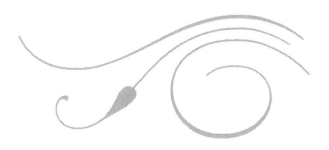

#6

Joy is . . .
the consequence of
making sure the good you do
over a lifetime
far outweighs
any hurt or harm
you may inadvertently cause.

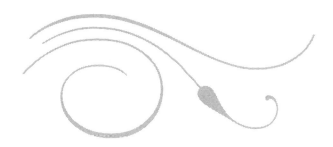

#7

Joy is . . .
discovering from experience
that imagination is indeed
the true magic.

#8

Joy is . . .
knowing that
the most special gift
you can give to a child
is your time.

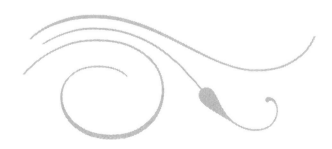

#9

Joy is . . .
having unwavering trust
in someone you love;
for without trust,
love cannot be
more than a fiery passion
unable to survive
precarious uncertainty.

#10

Joy is . . .
finding a way to avoid
the barrage of irritating distractions
that destroy inner serenity—
the pervasively pernicious phenomenon
that is our burden
from living in
a modern, technological society.

#11

Joy is . . .
successfully avoiding
serious overthinking
as much as is
humanly possible.

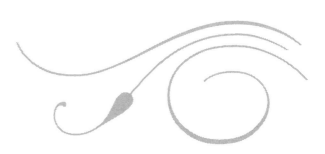

#12

Joy is . . .
believing that
the most sincere
and devout words of worship
won't move a person closer
to our Creator
as much as
actual deeds of compassion
in the real world.

#13

Joy is . . .
feeling completely at home
and relaxed
in your own skin,
regardless of where you are.

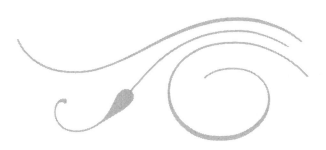

#14

Joy is . . .
personally beaming
a radiance of love
to those with whom
you interact each day.

#15

Joy is . . .
being clear,
consciously clear!

#16

Joy is . . .
resolutely mastering
the divine art of play.

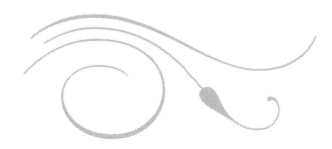

#17

Joy is . . .
having a network
of close friends and relatives
who deeply care about you,
who always will be there for you
in a crisis.

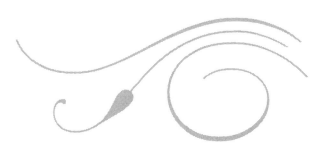

#18

Joy is . . .
knowing that courage is
the crucial fulcrum point
in the balance between
fear and foolishness.

#19

Joy is . . .
having arrived
at that special phase
in your personal development when,
rather than feeling discomfort with silence,
you find complete contentment and
fulfillment within it.

#20

Joy is . . .
living your life
with minimal regrets.

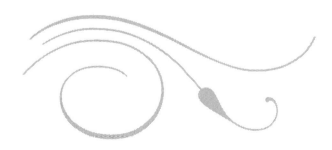

#21

Joy is . . .
quietly working at becoming
your own very-private hero.

#22

Joy is . . .
when you finally realize
the taste of really delicious,
but overly rich, food
is not as important,
in the fleeting moment of pleasuring,
as life itself.

#23

Joy is . . .
a prime benefit from
attaining and maintaining
ideal physical symmetry
between the left and right sides
of your body
and
energetic symmetry
between the left and right hemispheres
or your brain.

#24

Joy is . . .
the result
of humbly seeking
true humility.

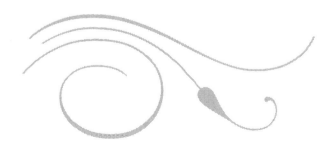

#25

Joy is . . .
resolving any neurotic tendencies
you may have,
so you can develop
healthy human relations
devoid of destructive defensiveness.

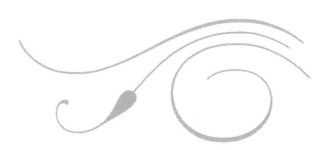

#26

Joy is . . .
holding peace in your heart
and
peace in your soul.

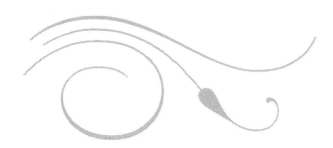

#27

Joy is . . .
the wisdom
of letting a child BE a child
as much as possible
and
guiding any essential form
of development
with very gentle,
encouraging support.

#28

Joy is . . .
working diligently to assure
that your long-term goal
of manifesting goodness
will always prevail.

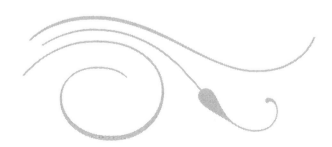

#29

Joy is . . .
having an astute belief
in the universal law
of cause and effect (karma);
that whatever you do
always comes back to you tenfold
and basic "intentionalily"
is at the core
of all karmic consequences.

#30

Joy is . . .
mindfully internalizing
the immense power
of positive thinking.

#31

Joy is . . .
when someone blesses you
with the parting wish,
"May you have enough!"
and you totally understand
the profound level of well-being
they are wanting for you to have.

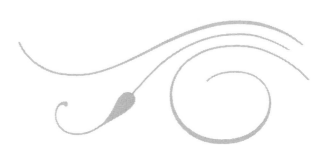

#32

Joy is . . .
being absolutely certain
that your spirit never dies.

#33

Joy is . . .
what happens
when you totally accept
two essential truths:
Life is inherently not perfect
and
life is not always fair.

#34

Joy is . . .
to consider yourself with modesty
and
view the world
with great sincerity and reverence.

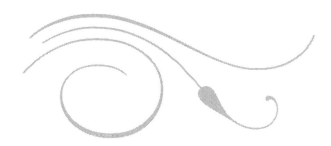

#35

Joy is . . .
understanding that healthy love
exists at the midpoint
between the extremes
of apathy and obsession.

#36

Joy is . . .
whenever you realize
that the "I" who is the enduring you
is not the physical body
people can outwardly see.

#37

Joy is . . .
comprehending
that your precious mind
is so much more
than just a servant
to the desire for pleasure.

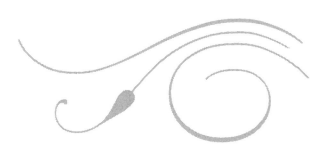

#38

Joy is . . .
when your mere presence
lifts people up
whenever you walk into a room.

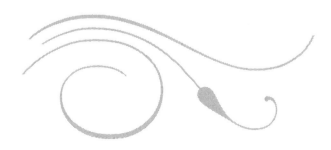

#39

Joy is . . .
living day to day
in such a conscious way
that you rarely have a need to say
you are sorry to anyone.

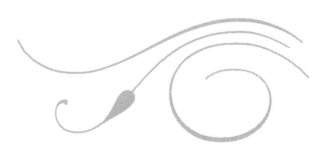

#40

Joy is . . .
appreciating a strict parental upbringing,
laced with high principles,
sterling integrity, and solid family values,
with a little tough love thrown in
whenever necessary.

#41

Joy is . . .
the end result
of being vigilant in preventing
your emotions
from destroying the harmony
and well-being
of your physical body.

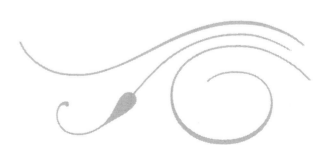

#42

Joy is . . .
the phenomenon of becoming
authentically and unapologetically
your basic "true self" more and more
as you get older.

#43

Joy is . . .
honoring the depth
of a parent's unconditional love,
clearly the most universal
comfort-generating force
known to humanity.

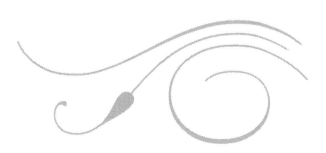

#44

Joy is . . .
wearing your healthy, humble,
confidence-boosting pride
on the inside,
so that it is cloistered
and unseen.

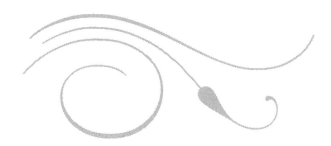

#45

Joy is . . .
knowing that sometimes
love is expressed
and sometimes it is not.

#46

Joy is . . .
understanding that
to speak only the truth
is the hallmark of an evolved old soul,
who knows well the consequences
of doing otherwise.

#47

Joy is . . .
standing in awe
of the most inscrutable mystery of all,
the spark of creation itself.

#48

Joy is . . .
knowing and navigating
the fine line
between discernment
and judgment.

#49

Joy is . . .
understanding that success
is really nothing more
than any job done well.

#50

Joy is . . .
discovering how
the act of letting go
of something you think
you know for certain
can open your eyes
to a newer
and, perhaps, more pertinent truth.

#51

Joy is . . .
learning that it is
not what you want to get
OUT of living that matters
as much as appreciating
whatever good
you already have
IN your life at the moment.

#52

Joy is . . .
the very pragmatic act
of
proactively seeking
wellness.

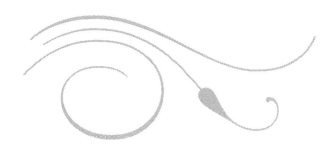

#53

Joy is . . .
expanding compassion
in your community
by personally distributing
that virtue freely
on a daily basis.

#54

Joy is . . .
having a strong commitment
to a distinctly higher code
of existence.

#55

Joy is . . .
getting a fair deal
and giving a fair deal in return,
so the universe can remain
in a perfect balance.

#56

Joy is . . .
what occurs
whenever you greet someone
with a hearty handshake
accompanied by
a steadfast look directly
into that person's eyes
and
then they reciprocate
in the same straightforward,
soul-binding manner.

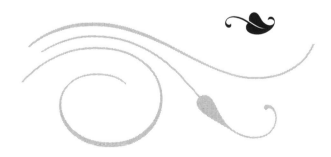

#57

Joy is . . .
believing that forever is not defined
by the number of times
a heart has left to beat.

#58

Joy is . . .
learning that
by growing up with very little
in the way of material things,
you more deeply appreciate
everything earned
through your own hard efforts.

#59

Joy is . . .
what happens when
you have abandoned the "me, me, me"
ego-based mind-set,
to be more inclusive of
the collective, filled
with "we, us, they, and them."

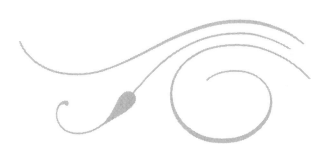

#60

Joy is . . .
being able to release
your pursuit of shallow desires
in deference to the next level of growth—
something called
a mature enrichment of the soul.

#61

Joy is . . .
having learned
that to worry excessively every day
is a surefire method
of reducing the number of days
left remaining
in which you can still worry.

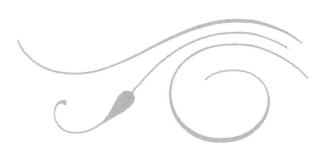

#62

Joy is . . .
whenever your thoughts
are truly worth much more
than just a penny,
especially as an elder.

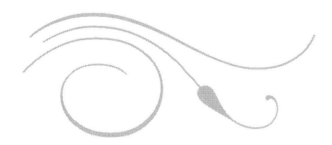

#63

Joy is . . .
the "suchness"
of being "tuned-in and turned-on"
to a new and more-beneficial paradigm
regarding what is essential for
your personal
evolution of consciousness.

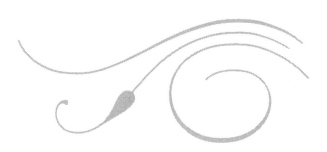

#64

Joy is . . .
having a few special friends
who always keep their word,
no matter what.

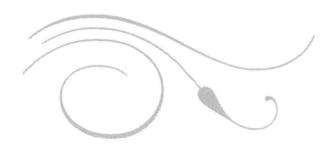

#65

Joy is . . .
treating all creatures kindly,
because each one is filled
with the same spirit
of the divine
as we,
their human cousins.

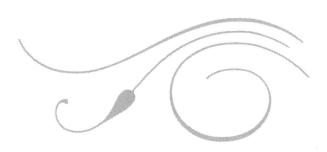

#66

Joy is . . .
that fleeting glimpse one gets
from time to time
of "Universal Love"
transcending
everyday consciousness.

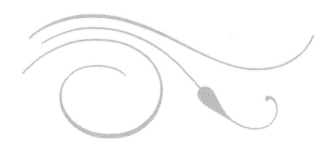

#67

Joy is . . .
what results from
anonymously giving
to any charity.

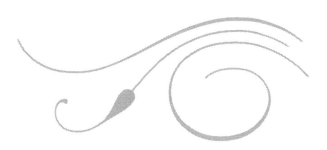

#68

Joy is . . .
becoming keenly aware
that the curious mind needs to discover
rather than be instructed.

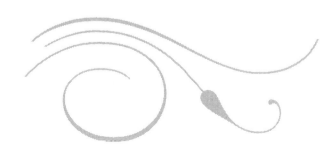

#69

Joy is . . .
inevitably found
within the formidable power
of unbridled optimism.

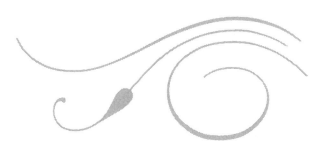

#70

Joy is . . .
successfully resolving
perhaps the most difficult Catch-22 of all:
to enjoy living in the sensual richness
of the material world
without getting overly attached to it.

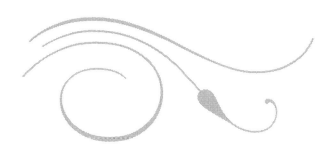

#71

Joy is . . .
realizing that vibrant participation
in the nuances of daily living
is the best panacea to prevent
passively dying
in a premature manner.

#72

Joy is . . .
when you arrive at a point of maturity,
where the word faster
is not such an essential part
of your vocabulary
as patience.

#73

Joy is . . .
the experience of unrequited love
steadily becoming
delightfully requited
over time.

#74

Joy is . . .
when you catch yourself
being unreasonably negative
and have the supreme presence of mind
to switch your attitude immediately.

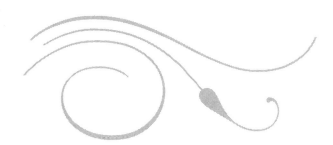

#75

Joy is . . .
having compassion
for those with a rebel heart,
who are learning from defiance
rather than compliance.

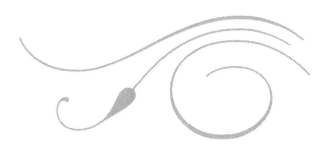

#76

Joy is . . .
routinely telling your "inner critic"
to take the day off,
because you are feeling really quite fine
about being uniquely and imperfectly
yourself.

#77

Joy is . . .
quietly promoting
planetary humanism.

#78

Joy is . . .
filling your days
with music, dance, song;
art and literature;
unrestrained laughter;
lots of long hugs, kisses,
and luscious intimacy
that collectively nourish
the soul.

#79

Joy is . . .
when you don't get what you wanted,
but instead get
what you really needed.

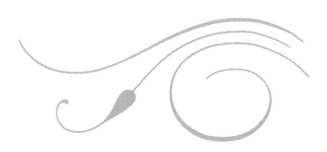

#80

Joy is . . .
living in harmony
with nature,
as part of nature.

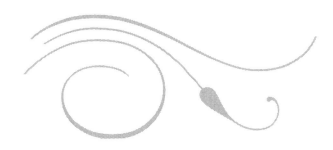

#81

Joy is . . .
realizing that
all the daily "trials and tribulations"
you encounter
are just master keys to a classroom
for your own, personal transformation
and potential enlightenment.

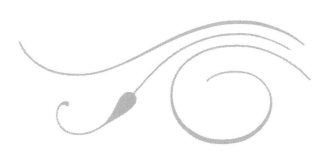

#82

Joy is . . .
when one has the epiphany
of seeing how everything and everyone
is connected
in some cryptic, metaphysical manner,
with varying degrees
of significance or insignificance.

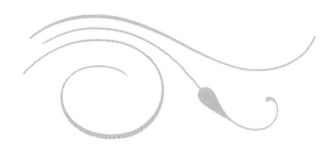

#83

Joy is . . .
having the freedom and willpower
to creatively forge
your own destiny.

#84

Joy is . . .
experiencing the nuances
of limitless love
gifted from
an enchantingly innocent child.

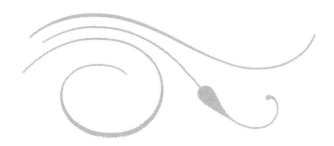

#85

Joy is . . .
having the insight to see
that the only way to move
past a troubling rough spot
is to give up your attachments
to your own treasured wounds.

#86

Joy is . . .
knowing that no amount
of physical attractiveness
will equal a heart
that is beautiful and pure.

#87

Joy is . . .
what occurs
whenever an honorable purpose
determines your ultimate reality.

#88

Joy is . . .
understanding
the wisdom of not manifesting
that old "eye-for-an-eye" mentality,
because it just ends up
leaving everyone without sight
and, even worse, without vision.

#89

Joy is . . .
listening to the wise guidance
and perspicacious revelations
of your inner dream maestro.

#90

Joy is . . .
the lesson learned by realizing
that when you meet someone
you intensely like or dislike,
both persons are equally compelling
mirrors
of who you are.

#91

Joy is . . .
experiencing the tranquility moment
of "being without thought,"
even if sustained
for only a few seconds.

#92

Joy is . . .
laying it all out there,
delivering the maximum effort
you are able to give each and every day,
so you will have no regrets
in your twilight years.

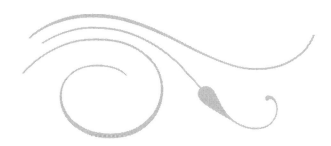

#93

Joy is . . .
treating your young son or daughter
like the adult
you hope they someday will be.

#94

Joy is . . .
always keeping commitments
you have made,
if for no better reason
than believing that
the veracity of one's word
is the hallmark of high moral integrity.

#95

Joy is . . .
fostering your reputation
as someone
who has a nurturing way of being.

#96

Joy is . . .
allowing a child
to teach you
that work can be play.

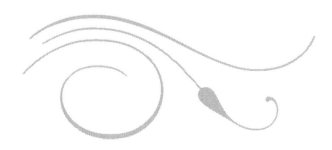

#97

Joy is . . .
expanding the "helping-others"
consciousness
exponentially;
after you have done a good deed for
somebody
and they ask how to repay the favor,
you request that the recipient
pass the good deed forward in like kind
to another person in need
at an opportune moment
in the future.

#98

Joy is . . .
happily splurging
on a little harmless self-indulgence
from time to time
with absolutely no recriminations,
whatsoever.

#99

Joy is . . .
realizing that it is often more beneficial
to see through the fresh eyes of a child,
because adults tend to overthink
the ordinary wonders
of the earth.

#100

Joy is . . .
cherishing all the blessings
and dear friends you have
before they mysteriously slip away
in time.

#101

Joy is . . .
the state of being naturally "high"
on the experience
of life itself!

#102

Joy is . . .
always feeling
sincere empathy for others
who have a more difficult
road to walk.

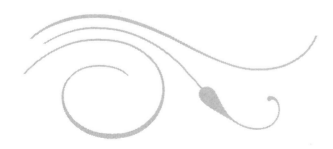

#103

Joy is . . .
discovering that
regardless of the conditions
in which you were raised,
if you believe in yourself,
you can accomplish just about anything.

#104

Joy is . . .
realizing that
your mental acuity determines
how much physical energy
you will have available
to do whatever is needed.

#105

Joy is . . .
happily fulfilling the promise
"to love, honor, and cherish" your spouse
forever,
then, as a couple,
collectively extending that same promise
to the rest of humanity.

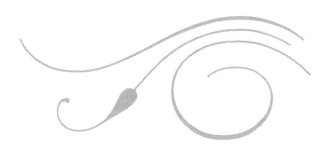

#106

Joy is . . .
one of the best rewards
from working
diligently each day
at having great stamina and flexibility.

#107

Joy is . . .
offering a supportive word
to someone in a serious crisis
who is crippled with worry and self-doubt.

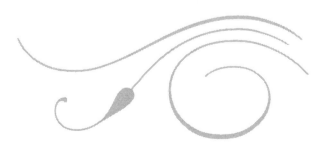

#108

Joy is . . .
aspiring to attain
a shame-free existence.

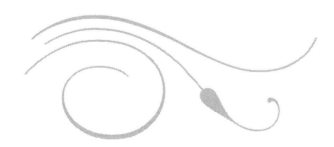

#109

Joy is . . .
grasping with astonishment
how much personal power you have
when you come up against
a dangerous situation
involving your most vulnerable self.

#110

Joy is . . .
tacitly accepting with a smile
that life goes on
in spite of you and because of you
with relative indifference.

#111

Joy is . . .
living spontaneously
and even breaking a few of the rules
along the way.

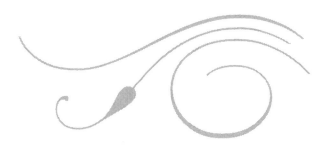

#112

Joy is . . .
having learned from experience
that a friend who understands your tears
is much more valuable
than scores of people
who have known only your mirth.

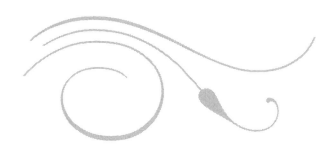

#113

Joy is . . .
being blessed
with solid and unbreakable
familial bonding.

#114

Joy is . . .
taking a chance on
something uncertain
because we generally regret
those opportunities we didn't take
much more than the ones we did.

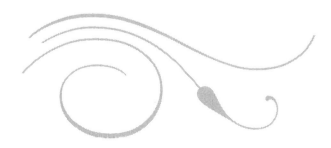

#115

Joy is . . .
the advisability of getting to know
the true "essential nature" of a person
over a long period of time
before entering into a
serious relationship
with that individual.

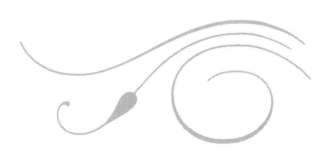

#116

Joy is . . .
having cheated death
and then making the most
of the new opportunity of life
given to you.

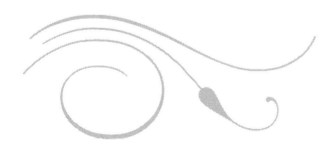

#117

Joy is . . .
making sure each day
to do no harm.

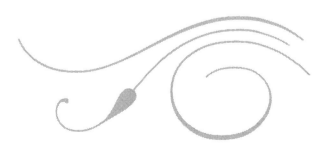

#118

Joy is . . .
when you envision someone
who has had many years filled
with love, adventure,
contribution, actualization,
growth, and contentment,
and then realize
that wonderful life is your own.

#119

Joy is . . .
seeing the paradox
of how
we all are both ordinary and unique
at the very same time.

#120

Joy is . . .
to be purposefully
more judicious with your words
in order to clearly demonstrate
the coherence of your thinking.

#121

Joy is . . .
making the commitment
to hone your heart-level skills
to their full potential.

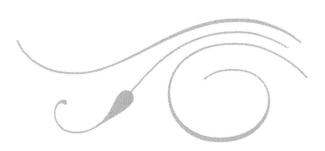

#122

Joy is . . .
sometimes not doing anything at all
when facing a serious dilemma,
because taking no action at all,
at times, can be
the best possible option.

#123

Joy is . . .
understanding
that having a long perspective
is a tremendous tool
for evolving to the apex
of your potentials.

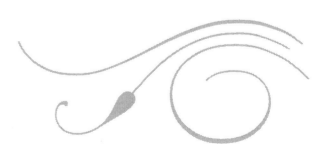

#124

Joy is . . .
speaking softly
so that you will be heard
more distinctly.

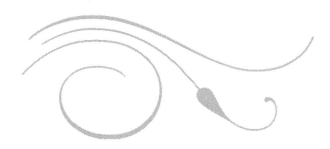

#125

Joy is . . .
seeing how youthfulness
is not just a phase of life
but, more notably, a state of mind.

#126

Joy is . . .
believing that luck
is, perhaps, nothing more
than probability
standing on its head
to attract attention.

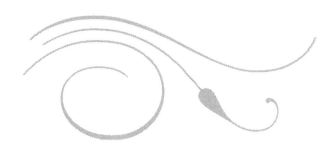

#127

Joy is . . .
not concerning yourself excessively
about troublesome matters
that you really don't have
the power or ability
to change.

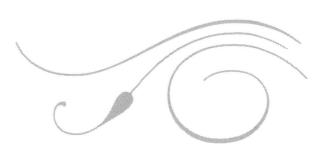

#128

Joy is . . .
discovering that,
when it comes to health and longevity,
what you eliminate from your diet
is often more beneficial
than what you add into it.

#129

Joy is . . .
what happens
when you are quick to forgive
and cautious to forget.

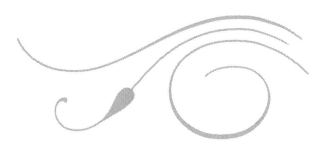

#130

Joy is . . .
standing tall,
no matter your own height
or that of your adversary.

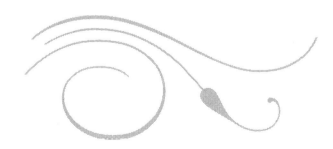

#131

Joy is . . .
the "aha" moment
when you realize
that one of the very best gifts
the past can bestow upon anyone
is character-redeeming hindsight.

#132

Joy is . . .
when you actualize the resolution
to not take yourself too seriously.

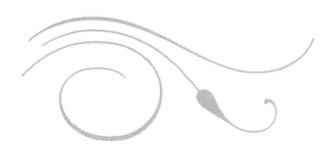

#133

Joy is . . .
the liberating process
of embracing serendipity
as a way to refresh your soul.

#134

Joy is . . .
when you have the awareness
to immediately sense those persons
who are destined to be
an insignificant part of your past
and those who will be
an integral part of your future.

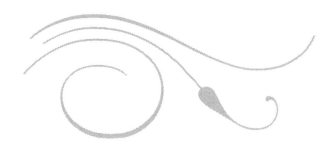

#135

Joy is . . .
slowing your body
and mind
into being quiescent.

#136

Joy is . . .
suddenly realizing
that you are probably a little better
than an overly critical self would
ever permit you to believe.

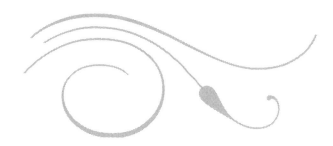

#137

Joy is . . .
discovering the immeasurable value
of practicing moderation in all things.

#138

Joy is . . .
approaching each day
with a beginner's mind
by always following your interests
with great enthusiasm,
precautionary alertness,
and a little naive boldness.

#139

Joy is . . .
living by the self-imposed doctrine
that your days should be filled with
one-third work, one-third play,
and one-third service to humanity,
equally implemented
with all the gusto
one can possibly generate.

#140

Joy is . . .
finding out the ironic secret
that true love rarely happens
when you frenetically look for it,
but more often occurs organically
when you stop seeking it
and dare to risk opening your heart.

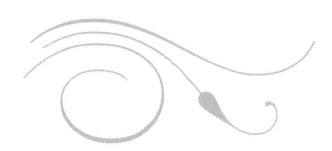

#141

Joy is . . .
being the kind of person
who speaks the truth,
even when you'd rather not.

#*142*

Joy is . . .
discovering with age
that the more you think you know,
the less you can comprehend.

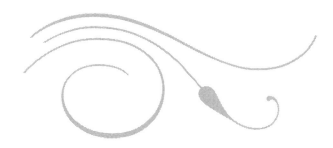

#143

Joy is . . .
always treating people
who are less educated,
intelligent, or fortunate
than you
with great kindness and respect,
for to do so,
ennobles and enriches you both.

#144

Joy is . . .
understanding
that taking affirmative action
is the difference between
getting what you want
and getting whatever fate happens
to drop in your lap.

#145

Joy is . . .
knowing from experience
that, in the long run,
the rejuvenating peace of obscurity
may be more valuable
than the transitory thrill
of notoriety and fame.

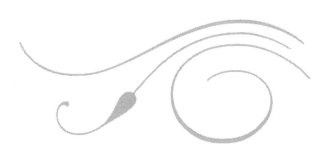

#146

Joy is . . .
not taking yourself too seriously,
because all of creation
is ultimately one continuous
divine comedy.

#147

Joy is . . .
when the odds are greater
than one-in-a-million
for a good thing to happen to someone
and you happen to be
that very "one" individual.

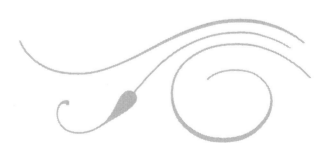

#148

Joy is . . .
finding out from experience
that to be afraid to fail is quite normal,
but to be afraid to try, so unwise.

#149

Joy is . . .
knowing that regular exercise
is truly
the ultimate fountain of youth.

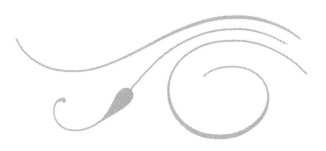

#150

Joy is . . .
the subtle promise of today
as a blank page
in a book of blank pages.

#151

Joy is . . .
caring for others
without expecting
anything in return.

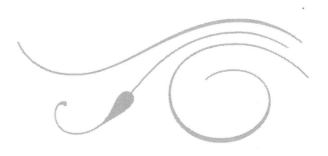

#152

Joy is . . .
appreciating how all the individuals
within your complex social networks
have impacted you
in some meaningful manner.

#153

Joy is . . .
treating everyone you first meet
as if each individual were
your long lost friend,
because someday
those individuals just may be.

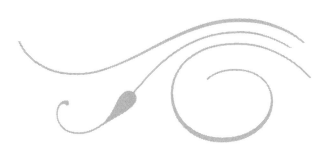

#154

Joy is . . .
discovering the ancient truth
that the successful endurance of time
is directly related
to simplicity.

#155

Joy is . . .
what happens
when you cherish
the people in your life
more than the things in your life.

#156

Joy is . . .
when you receive some
unforeseen riches
that are not of the material kind,
thus making them
so much more worthwhile.

#157

Joy is . . .
being totally obsessed, beguiled,
dazzled, spellbound, charmed, smitten,
captivated, bonkers, bewitched,
mesmerized, and hopelessly
head-over-heels in love
with the person of your dreams,
and the feeling
just gets stronger every day
and better in every way.

#158

Joy is . . .
seeing the more principled aspects
of yourself
reflected in the actions and personality
of your own child.

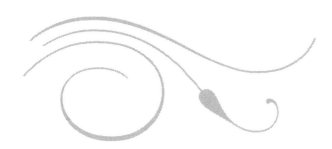

#159

Joy is . . .
when your memories of the good times
are substantial enough
to sustain you when
you can no longer "do,"
but are bound by circumstance
to "just be."

#160

Joy is . . .
having the wisdom
to prevent a catastrophe
with foresight and preparedness.

#161

Joy is . . .
receiving divine grace
when you least expect it.

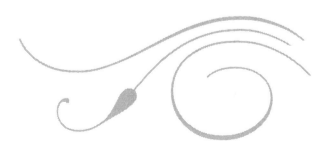

#162

Joy is . . .
finally coming to the awareness
that those who truly understand you
may be very few
amongst the many people
you encounter through the years,
but the few are enough.

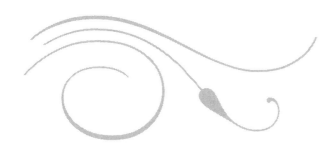

#163

Joy is . . .
forever honoring your parents
for the obvious reality that,
without them,
the "I" who is you,
body-mind and spirit,
simply would not be.

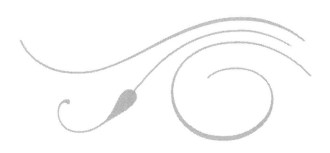

#164

Joy is . . .
setting a personal protocol
so that,
whenever you initially meet someone,
you first look for the attribute
of innate beauty within that individual.

#165

Joy is . . .
discovering that time runs faster
than we can possibly chase it,
so it is best to roll
with the flow of now.

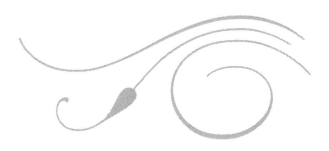

#166

Joy is . . .
that exquisite time of quiet after,
with heart pounding wildly,
punctuated by little sighs,
the stroking of skin,
and the forming of turned-up corners
of an almost grin,
in complete satisfaction
with the intimate universe
of soul-fusion ecstasy.

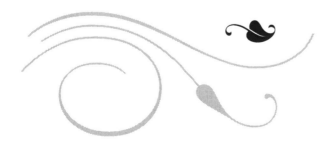

#167

Joy is . . .
living by the principle
that it is not so much
what you say that counts,
but what you do.

#168

Joy is . . .
being blessed with the ability
to drop into euphoric,
uninterrupted sleep
whenever you wish
and
to do so regularly
for a full measure of rejuvenation
each night.

#169

Joy is . . .
when your primary,
essential inclination
is to be giving
rather than taking.

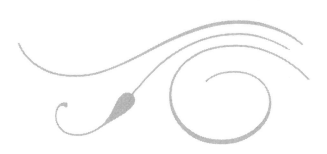

#170

Joy is . . .
having reached a point
where one does not require great luxury
in order to be happy,
or self-fulfilled.

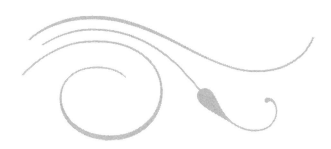

#171

Joy is . . .
the personal peace in believing
that the best revenge
is to not do anything at all,
allowing the law of karma
to settle the score,
because revenge, in and of itself,
creates its own negative karma.

#172

Joy is . . .
when a well-intentioned
and brutally honest friend
offers an unsolicited,
eye-opening observation
about a vexatious behavior you exhibit
that you had not previously considered,
and you are grateful.

#173

Joy is . . .
knowing in your heart
that to do the right thing
is never wrong.

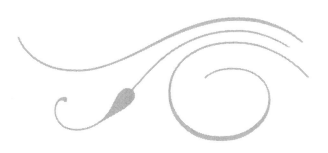

#174

Joy is . . .
devoutly believing that
we all come into this world
for a purpose
and
then finding out, without a doubt,
what your reason for being is.

#175

Joy is . . .
allowing adventuresome exploration
to bring newness and spice
into your daily experience.

#176

Joy is . . .
doing something selfless
in order to create great happiness
in another.

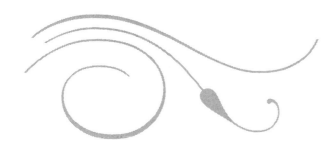

#177

Joy is . . .
listening very carefully
when you have the insight
to ask your mother and father
what they sacrificed in their lives
to take on the role of parenthood.

#178

Joy is . . .
when you attain the wisdom
to honor and embrace
those disowned and disliked
aspects of your inner selves.

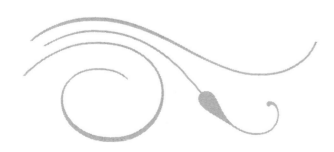

#179

Joy is . . .
being able to actually appreciate
the opportunity
for you to learn about forgiveness
at a higher level
from those who have hurt you somehow
with their unkind, callous behavior.

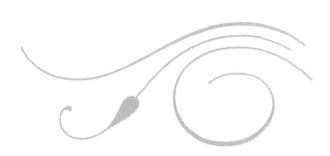

#180

Joy is . . .
when excellence becomes
the expected norm
for your daily aspirations.

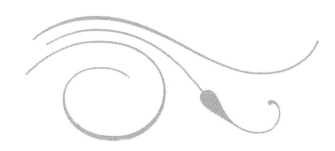

#181

Joy is . . .
knowing that the most
significant wealth
is not really measured
by money or physical assets,
but more by a nebulous currency
of the heart.

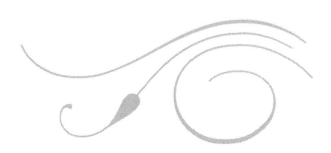

#182

Joy is . . .
being able to actively control
your daily choice
between eating food for its fuel value
and
eating food just for pleasure.

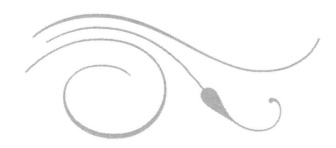

#183

Joy is . . .
what comes from heeding
timeless biblical wisdom
and successfully avoiding
the seven deadly sins
of pride, greed, lust, envy,
gluttony, wrath, and sloth.

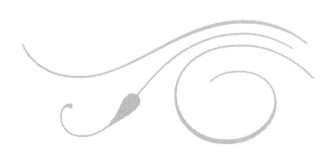

#184

Joy is . . .
having at least one good friend
with a very sympathetic ear
in difficult times.

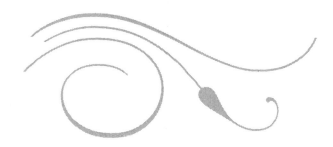

#185

Joy is . . .
the moment when
you've had a huge argument
with someone you care about,
then gracefully accept and admit
that you were totally,
one-hundred percent wrong.

#186

Joy is . . .
humbly emulating
those poor people who own little,
but will give you the shirt off their back
if you need it.

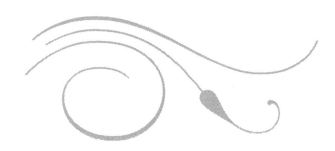

#187

Joy is . . .
being true to your word
along with everything
that your positive actions
honestly create.

#188

Joy is . . .
when you need nothing
and want nothing,
so that you are someone for whom
to buy a present is completely
impossible—
a very good thing indeed!

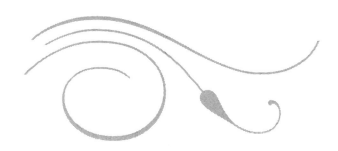

#189

Joy is . . .
appreciating the long-term benefits
of the four "r's"—
repetition, rhythm, regularity, and
routine—
truly stabilizing forces that
provide one with the security
to step outside the box
from time to time.

#190

Joy is . . .
understanding
that a winner
is generally someone
who never gives up trying
until success is attained.

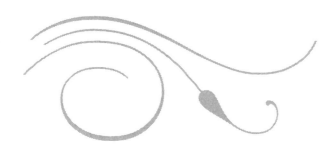

#191

Joy is . . .
exhibiting the discipline
to live within your means
and having the prudence
to "save for a rainy day."

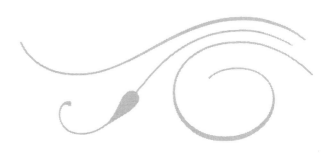

#192

Joy is . . .
quietly becoming an adept observer
so as to not be
a weary slave
to your own boundless thoughts.

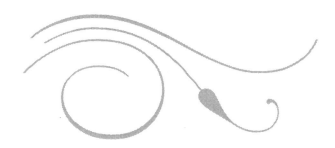

#193

Joy is . . .
knowing that those
who are loved best
can love others even better.

#194

Joy is . . .
kinesthetically feeling
the rejuvenating power
of stillness.

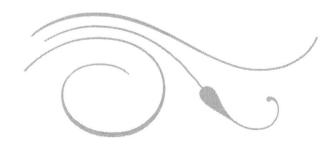

#195

Joy is . . .
when you truly believe in miracles
and then observe them
blooming all around you.

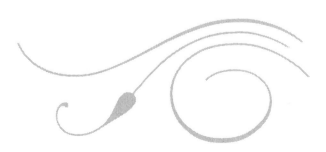

#196

Joy is . . .
kicking back with someone
who totally "gets you"
and who demands
nothing from you.

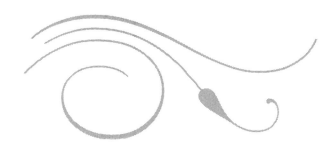

#197

Joy is . . .
confidently engaging others
with no pretentiousness.

#198

Joy is . . .
letting silence speak for you,
before you ever open your mouth.

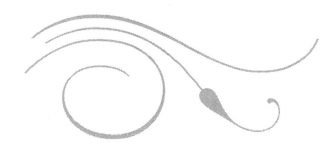

#199

Joy is . . .
seeing an elderly couple
walking hand in hand in the park,
inspiring hope
for everlasting marital bliss.

#200

Joy is . . .
taking a precarious leap of faith
and sticking the landing.

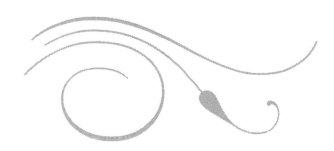

#201

Joy is . . .
having the epiphany
that energy follows thought
and then observing
that fundamental law in action.

#202

Joy is . . .
absolute freedom
from any falsehood.

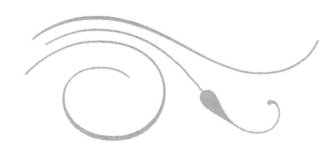

#203

Joy is . . .
never allowing
someone's biased opinion
to unduly shape your own reality.

#204

Joy is . . .
going all in and winning big,
not at the gaming tables,
but in life itself.

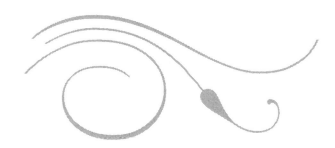

#205

Joy is . . .
thinking with lucidity
in a crucial, decisive moment.

#206

Joy is . . .
always being an enthusiastic
and attentive student
in the school of life,
regardless of your age.

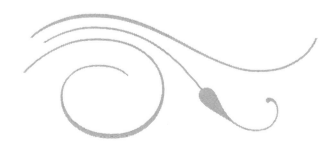

#207

Joy is . . .
choosing friends
who basically don't know how to make
fake smiles.

#208

Joy is . . .
being filled with greater curiosity
than a single lifetime
would allow anyone to satisfy.

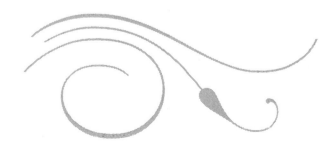

#209

Joy is . . .
realizing that you are who you are today
as much because
of your many mistakes along the way,
as of your valued achievements.

#210

Joy is . . .
being a positive role model for others
in a quiet way,
with no hidden expectations or intentions,
other than holding true
to who you are.

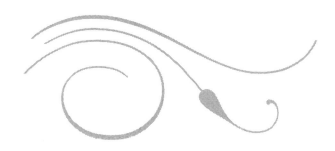

#211

Joy is . . .
passing through life
without any addictions
and
having great empathy for those who
are not so fortunate.

#212

Joy is . . .
when you orchestrate your days
to be forever young
and free in spirit.

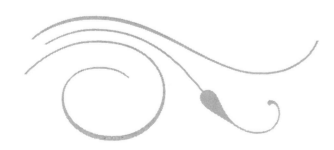

#213

Joy is . . .
successfully managing
your financial affairs
so money is not a stressful issue
of major concern.

#214

Joy is . . .
communicating effectively,
by not "babbling" in your own head
when you should be listening.

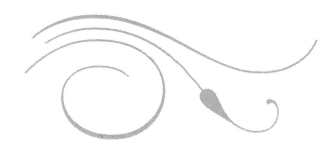

#215

Joy is . . .
manifesting a passionate desire
to safeguard the environment
for future generations.

#216

Joy is . . .
understanding
that sustaining
a passionately tenacious effort
toward an attainable goal
is the primary precursor to success.

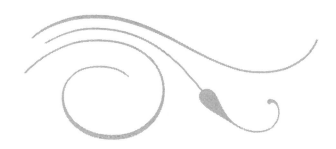

#217

Joy is . . .
swinging along with the pendulum
of life's ticking clock
and hanging on tight
as it hits the extremes of the arc.

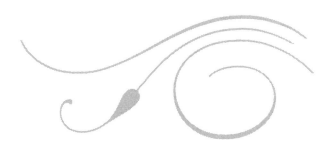

#218

Joy is . . .
cultivating the invaluable skill
of remaining detached
and devoid of affect
in the appropriate moments.

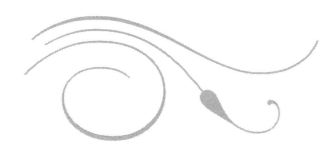

#219

Joy is . . .
realizing the inherent hope in the fact
that as long as you have
one day
with breath remaining,
you still have, at least,
one last opportunity
to change who you are.

#220

Joy is . . .
understanding that
plain old "common sense"
cannot be taught to you,
but is something that you must discover
and acquire on your own.

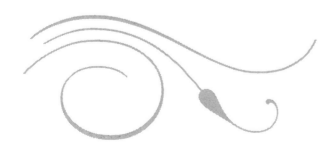

#221

Joy is . . .
having learned
that the difference between
trying to do the clearly possible
and succeeding with
the seemingly impossible
is the elementary knack
of believing in yourself.

#222

Joy is . . .
living a virtuous existence,
because ultimately
we always look back.

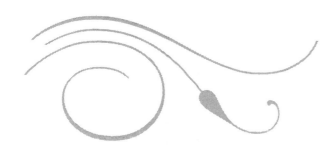

#223

Joy is . . .
slowing down enough
to discover the wonderful
nuances of beauty
that abound all around you.

#224

Joy is . . .
understanding the importance
of exercising your mind
as well as your body,
especially as you age.

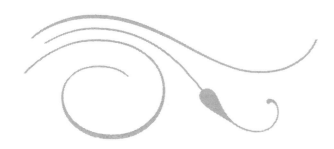

#225

Joy is . . .
when fate throws you a curve,
and you knock it out of the park.

#226

Joy is . . .
realizing that
one must experience some hardships
in order to truly appreciate
the high points of living.

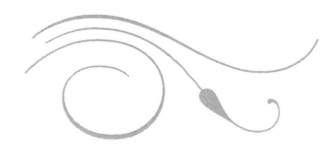

#227

Joy is . . .
sustaining a supportive,
loving relationship
that continually completes you
over many, many decades.

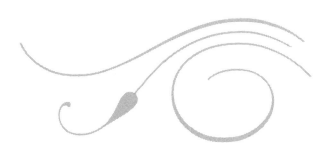

#228

Joy is . . .
showing, not telling,
your child how to be creative.

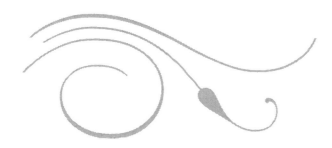

#229

Joy is . . .
never forgetting
that happily married couples
often live longer
and that those wedded folks
who are not so happy
live shorter lives
that only seem longer.

#230

Joy is . . .
naturally having a "can-do" attitude
with whatever challenge you face.

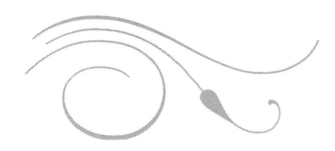

#231

Joy is . . .
realizing that,
perhaps, the most difficult thing
to do each day
is to be authentic
as yourself.

#232

Joy is . . .
knowing you never need to regret
being kind to someone,
regardless of what they do
with that kindness.

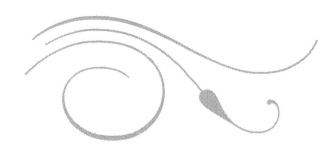

#233

Joy is . . .
when you have successfully handled
the difficult traumas of your youth
and turned those "bumps in the road"
into the quintessential lessons
making you a better person.

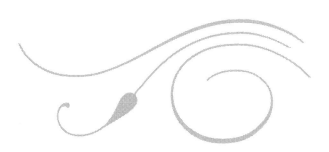

#234

Joy is . . .
responsibility taken seriously
as a measure of your worth.

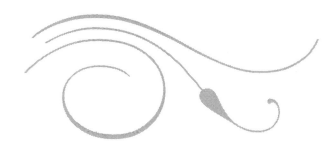

#235

Joy is . . .
allowing your fantasies
to run away with you
and lead you to wondrous, new places.

#236

Joy is . . .
the warm sense of fulfillment one gets
when vocation and occupation
are fused as one.

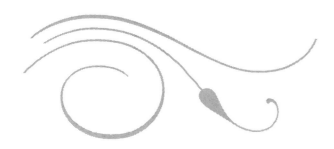

#237

Joy is . . .
mastering the most difficult
language of all,
the one with which you always speak
the absolute truth.

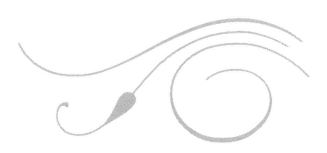

#238

Joy is . . .
waking up each morning
with the ardent intent
of finding goodness
at least once
during your day.

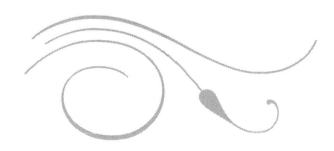

#239

Joy is . . .
faithfully being
a very loyal friend.

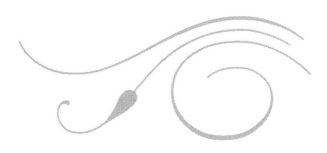

#240

Joy is . . .
when providence gives you
a second chance
to do something right,
and you do,
do it right.

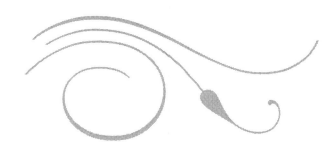

#241

Joy is . . .
the phenomenon of
hearing with more sensitive ears
and seeing with keener eyes
as you navigate
the spiritual realms.

#242

Joy is . . .
what happens when you give yourself
time to think before you take action
on an issue of consequence.

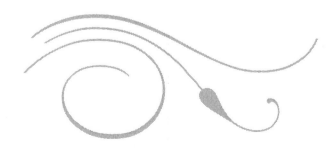

#243

Joy is . . .
clearly seeing the ironic
and humorous parallels
between the profound
and the mundane.

#244

Joy is . . .
having the wisdom
to effectively balance
the energy one spends
on benefitting the planet
with the time spent
on more personal pursuits.

#245

Joy is . . .
trusting your intuition
when your logical mind
offers doubtful solutions!

#246

Joy is . . .
viewing imperfection
as the impetus
to whatever moves us
forward.

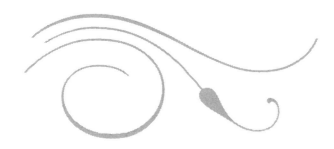

#247

Joy is . . .
seeing that
any obstacle you encounter
on your path
IS your path.

#248

Joy is . . .
making sure
when starting any relationship,
that ethnicity is never a factor
of relevance or importance.

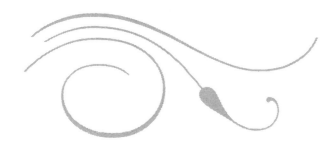

#249

Joy is . . .
what happens
when what goes on in your head
aligns with the talk you talk
and the walk you walk.

#250

Joy is . . .
knowing how to ask the right question
in order to
find the right answer.

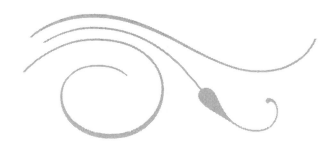

#251

Joy is . . .
giving a helping hand
to make a special wish come true
for a total stranger.

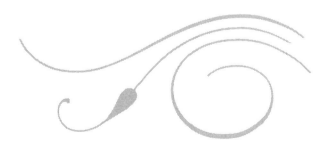

#252

Joy is . . .
whenever you encounter
understated eloquence
in an unlikely place.

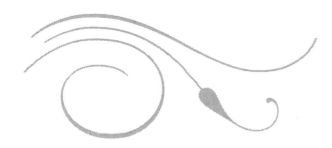

#253

Joy is . . .
resourceful learning
by intuitively doing.

#254

Joy is . . .
realizing that
if you can dream it,
you can do it.

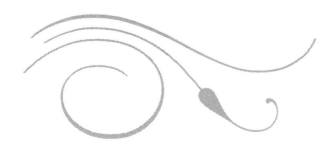

#255

Joy is . . .
understanding that
significant karmic lessons
repeat themselves
until they are finally learned.

#256

Joy is . . .
seeking to cultivate
an artist's eye and aesthetics
when designing your own living space,
because where you dwell
is a reflection of your inner soul:
valuable hint,
less is best!

#257

Joy is . . .
when real contentment
becomes
a common, everyday experience.

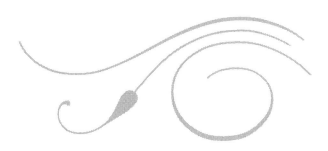

#258

Joy is . . .
having the conviction that
all it takes to make someone feel special
is to help that person believe
they already are,
then that person will become
what they believe.

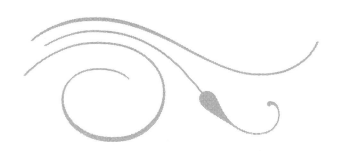

#259

Joy is . . .
quietly worshipping all alone
in the most magnificent temple of all,
unspoiled nature.

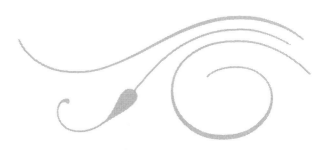

#260

Joy is . . .
faithfully abiding
by your own solid, core beliefs
and not compromising them
for anyone,
for any reason.

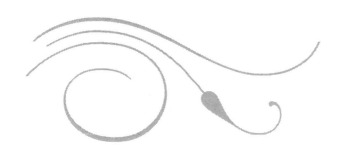

#261

Joy is . . .
being of the opinion that
allowing a placid lull from speaking
is much better
than uttering a litany of empty words
to senselessly fill a void.

#262

Joy is . . .
internalizing the awareness
that negativity brings fewer years
and positivity equals more years
in which to enjoy the gift of life.

#263

Joy is . . .
demonstrating selfless generosity
whenever you can.

#264

Joy is . . .
what occurs
when you live the motto,
"Loving life to the max!"

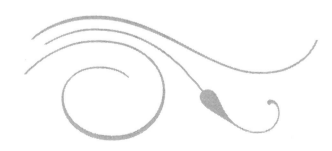

#265

Joy is . . .
seeing that
when too many obstacles
are blocking your way,
some unknown benevolent force
may be trying to protect you
by keeping you safe from danger.

#266

Joy is . . .
discovering what every sailor knows:
The set of the sail
and not the force of the gale
is what determines where you go.

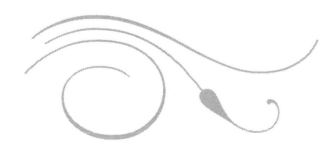

#267

Joy is . . .
being okay with solitary time
because it gives to you
a unique kind of power
unknown to most people.

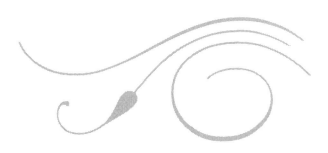

#268

Joy is . . .
judiciously knowing
when to reveal information
and when to discreetly
keep certain things unspoken.

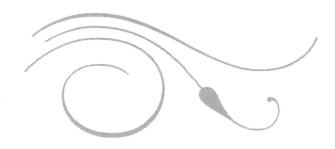

#269

Joy is . . .
what happens
whenever you engage people
with an intentionality of acceptance.

#270

Joy is . . .
carefully listening
whenever your body speaks.

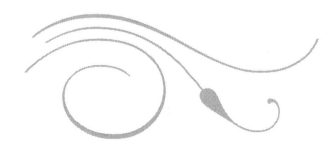

#271

Joy is . . .
realizing that
living up to your full potential
is a bold escapade
that often involves taking a big gamble
for an uncertain reward.

#272

Joy is . . .
realizing that
fighting force with force
is not the only way to prevail,
with notable exceptions.

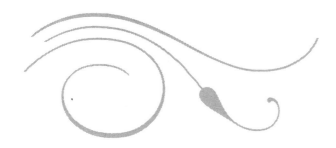

#273

Joy is . . .
carefully cultivating
your own perpetual
inner smile of harmony.

#274

Joy is . . .
having a loving relationship partner
upon whom one can rely
through thick and thin,
regardless of the situation.

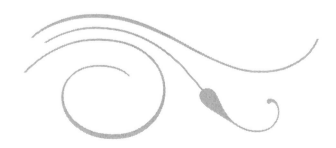

#275

Joy is . . .
being the cheerful donor
of many small acts of contagious kindness
each and every day.

#276

Joy is . . .
taking an equitable, "quid pro quo"
(something for something)
approach to living.

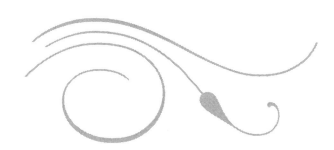

#277

Joy is . . .
striving to be known
not only as
a thinker and a scholar,
but as a lover
of all the diverse inhabitants on this
spinning, little haven
for life in the universe.

#278

Joy is . . .
standing with honorable principles,
unwavering and unbendable
against the forces
of evil, injustice,
tyranny, and oppression,
just as any self-respecting
superhero would do.

#279

Joy is . . .
having learned
that the only way to find out
how far you can really go
is to go beyond
how far you thought you might go
and then
never stop moving forward!

#280

Joy is . . .
inherent in the wisdom
acquired by quietly doubting
and objectively questioning
everything,
because reality is quite possibly
just an illusion.

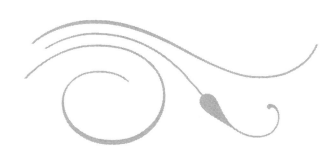

#281

Joy is . . .
discovering how to successfully release
the negative, stressful energies
one inevitably feels from encountering
the dangerous survival challenges
facing our civilization today.

#282

Joy is . . .
the liberating confidence
that comes naturally
when your intentions
are transparent and honest.

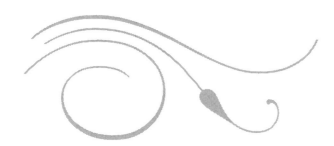

#283

Joy is . . .
believing that
ſrom the darkness came the light
and a spot of light always exists
somewhere within the darkness.

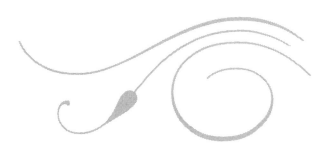

#284

Joy is . . .
having initial trust
for just about everyone
until they give you a reason
to not do so.

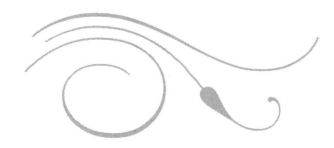

#285

Joy is . . .
appreciating something
which radically alters
everything you once believed
and gives to you
a completely new perspective.

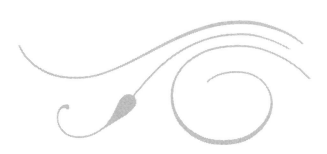

#286

Joy is . . .
knowing that each day you are alive
is a precious gift
more valuable
than any material treasure
or transitory pleasure.

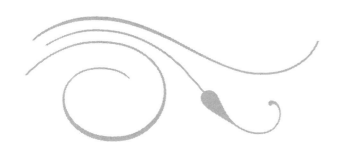

#287

Joy is . . .
developing your ordinary ego
into an "aware" ego,
for the conscious management
of the rich cast of inner-selves
dwelling within you.

#288

Joy is . . .
giving the gift of hope to another
in that individual's darkest hour.

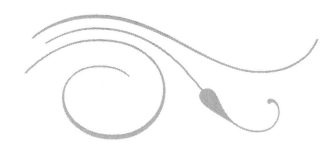

#289

Joy is . . .
always staying actively involved
with a relevant purpose each day,
because you are aware
that succumbing to apathy
surely will reduce the number
of your years
and certainly render them
not as appealing.

#290

Joy is . . .
realizing that enlightenment
is nothing more than being at one with
the noble expectations
of an unseen organizing intelligence
much wiser than yourself.

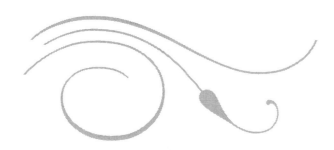

#291

Joy is . . .
cultivating the attribute of letting go
in order to liberate yourself
from the tremendous energy wasted
by holding on
to long-term emotional baggage.

#292

Joy is . . .
living a bountiful existence
with mindful temperance.

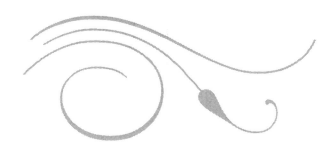

#293

Joy is . . .
making sure that all the gifts you give
come from the heart,
with no strings attached.

#294

Joy is . . .
intently working
at keeping all the
subtle energy systems in the body
well nurtured, balanced, fully
"charged," and circulating freely.

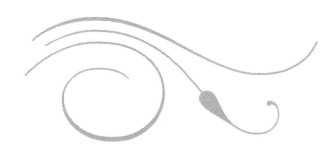

#295

Joy is . . .
benefitting from
the covert, symbolic power
of recurring dreams.

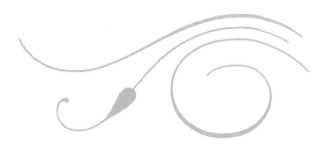

#296

Joy is . . .
knowing for certain
that selfless service to others
carries you
to divine enchantment.

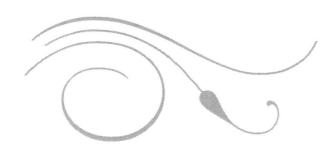

#297

Joy is . . .
demurely becoming a master,
without ever seeking to be one.

#298

Joy is . . .
appreciating what cultural
diversity brings
to the table of social evolution.

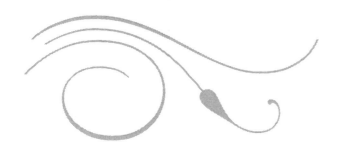

#299

Joy is . . .
always being your own boss
because you can't be fired
if you make a mistake.

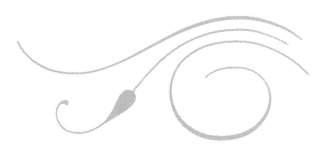

#300

Joy is . . .
loving yourself enough
to genuinely like yourself.

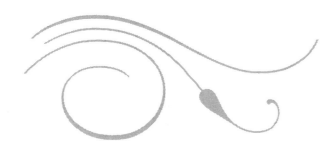

#301

Joy is . . .
fighting against greed,
corruption, and power,
and WINNING!!!

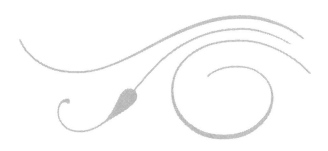

#302

Joy is . . .
living a guilt-free existence.

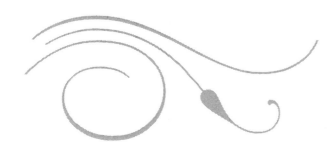

#303

Joy is . . .
being adventuresome enough
to try just about anything
at least once.

#304

Joy is . . .
when you explicitly set your intent
on being accountable
for all your actions.

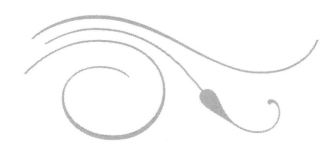

#305

Joy is . . .
what occurs
when your view of what is essential
goes beyond the acquisition
of material things.

#306

Joy is . . .
keeping those people close
who really "get" who you are
and are motivated
to stay and support you
along your personal journey.

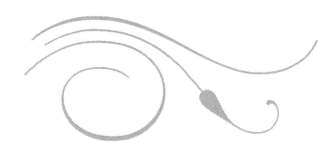

#307

Joy is . . .
cheerfully honoring
all the obligations
and commitments you've made,
regardless of the changing conditions
created by circumstance.

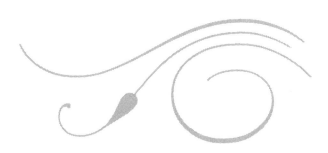

#308

Joy is . . .
when you feel completely confident
upon first meeting anyone,
regardless of that person's status, title,
fortune, or fame,
because you live with the knowledge that
we are all just the same
carbon-, hydrogen-, nitrogen-,
and phosphorus-based life-form!

#309

Joy is . . .
focusing on
the heart center
as the place from which
you can best engage others.

#310

Joy is . . .
being aware
that negative "reactiveness"
coming from someone else
is generally the consequence
of your own judgmental mind-set.

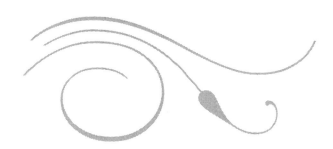

#311

Joy is . . .
to create inner alignment,
balance, and equilibrium
in mind, body, and spirit.

#312

Joy is . . .
discovering that
if you possess great knowledge
but no spirituality or love,
you have the least of all.

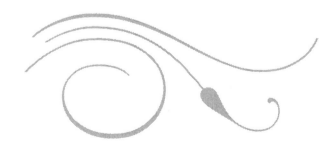

#313

Joy is . . .
learning that
if you see with only your eyes
and not your heart,
you can easily be deceived.

#314

Joy is . . .
having a special quiet haven
where you can go
to sort things out on a regular basis.

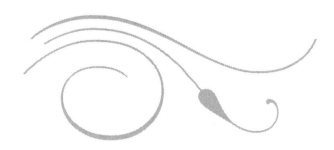

#315

Joy is . . .
learning from experience
that creativity fosters success.

#316

Joy is . . .
the contagious overflow of positivity
that results from intentionally focusing
solely on all the caring
and good deeds
you witness in the world,
with the conscious exclusion of
everything else.

#317

Joy is . . .
something as very elemental
as getting up each morning
with the firm commitment
to do the best that you can do
with whatever is on your agenda
that day.

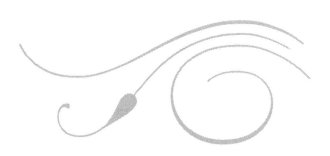

#318

Joy is . . .
finding a way to absolve yourself
for all the foolish and unconscious things
you did in your past,
so you will be free to live
emotionally unencumbered
in the present.

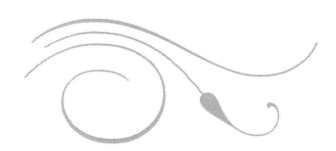

#319

Joy is . . .
when empowerment comes organically
from walking the path
that suits you best.

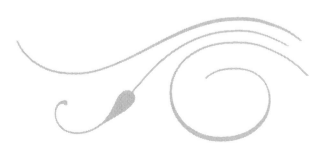

#320

Joy is . . .
discovering obsessive desires
to be the most common flaw
diverting any individual
from the quest for true happiness.

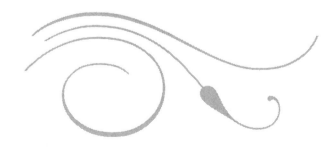

#321

Joy is . . .
feeling completely at ease
with the reality
that you will never know
as much as you wish you could know.

#322

Joy is . . .
seeing that the way
in which you resonate
with your outer surroundings
determines your inner-reality
and certainly your inner-peace.

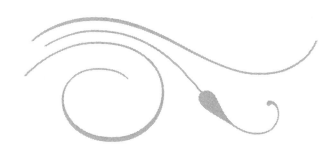

#323

Joy is . . .
experiencing the benefits
of staying "impersonal"
when at the center
of any personal conflict.

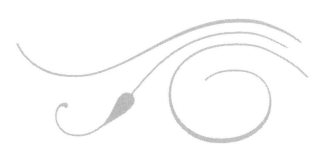

#324

Joy is . . .
having learned
that if achieving a major goal
comes too easily,
that success often doesn't mean as much
as accomplishing the same thing
through struggle, hard work,
and perseverance.

#325

Joy is . . .
humbly appreciating,
in your own reverent way,
the ethereal force
responsible for creating the universe.

#326

Joy is . . .
realizing that you can't
expect your friends
to be exactly like you,
lest you be left with but one friend,
yourself.

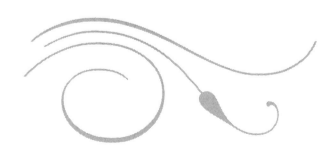

#327

Joy is . . .
becoming aware
that envy is truly pointless
and, ultimately,
a very destructive flaw
of the primitive ego.

#328

Joy is . . .
knowing that it is wiser
to fall in love
with the soul of a person
than the ephemeral attractive face
with which they happened to be blessed
merely by chance.

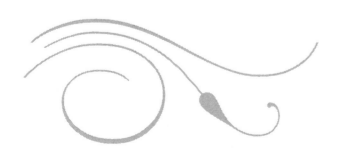

#329

Joy is . . .
having a dedicated moral obligation
to your own self-generated
ethical doctrine
of
what is right.

#330

Joy is . . .
when it doesn't matter
what you are doing
as long as it is with
the one you love.

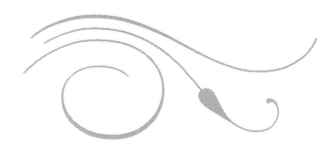

#331

Joy is . . .
completely avoiding
an ambitious quest for power, might,
and domination,
because such an intent usually leads to
delusion, disappointment,
and discontent.

#332

Joy is . . .
knowing that the most meaningful thing
in effective communication is
hearing what is not being
said in the words
spoken by someone.

#333

Joy is . . .
understanding the profound implications
of the reality
that change/impermanence
is the only real constant in the universe
and, ultimately,
ours is always the task of continual
adjustment and adaptation.

#334

Joy is . . .
passionately learning
as much as you can,
about everything you can,
whenever you possibly can.

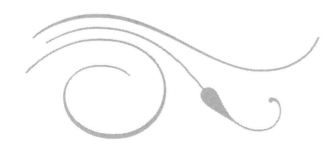

#335

Joy is . . .
when a man feels completely comfortable
revealing emotional vulnerability,
without concerns
of being viewed as weak.

#336

Joy is . . .
when a woman can stand
strong and powerful,
yet still be deemed feminine.

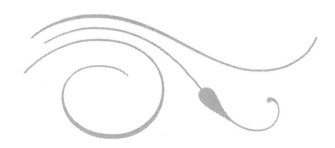

#337

Joy is . . .
when you defy all the odds and win,
because destiny is not determined
by statistical probabilities,
and thus,
your future holds available to you
infinite possibilities.

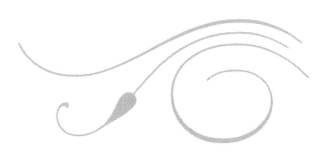

#338

Joy is . . .
never sweating
the problematic "small stuff" in life
and recognizing that,
if money can fix a situation,
then that circumstance most likely isn't
such a critical issue
in the larger scheme of things.

#339

Joy is . . .
the intrinsic reward you receive
from hosting a regular weekly meal,
a time set aside as a special gathering
with those whom you treasure the most,
so you can keep the bonds of love
alive and precious.

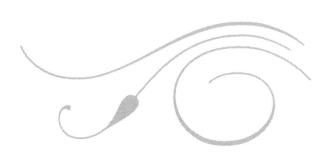

#340

Joy is . . .
being able to avoid the common flaw
of viewing people
with distorted "bipolar eyes,"
which divides all humanity
into "them and us."

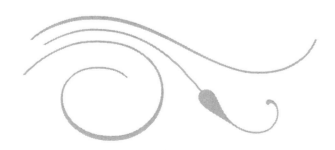

#341

Joy is . . .
realizing that active people
tend to stay that way
and live the longest;
inactive people
tend to stay that way
and are more likely
to depart prematurely.

#342

Joy is . . .
being especially aware of
the fundamental reality that
approximately
sixty percent of our body mass is water
and that one of the most powerful,
yet often neglected, practices
so vital for attaining good
health is hydrating ourselves
with an ample amount of clear, pure water
each and every day,
for water is life.

#343

Joy is . . .
believing that our best shot at immortality
is the enduring legacy we leave
in the hearts of those people
we have somehow touched
in a significant way.

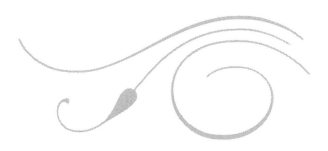

#344

Joy is . . .
being cautious with our words,
for they are like arrows:
once released into the air,
those potentially lethal, pointed shafts
are forever out of our control.

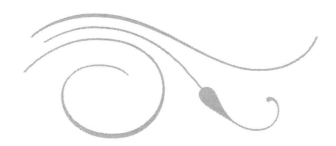

#345

Joy is . . .
realizing that
when somebody enters your social circle
with whom you have a strong
energetic connection,
that individual will most likely be
of great relevance
to your grand karmic resolution.

#346

Joy is . . .
having learned from experience
that if you have few material possessions,
you value your very existence
and the people close to you
more greatly.

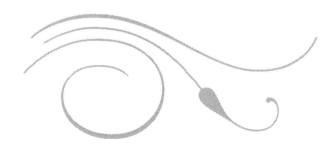

#347

Joy is . . .
understanding that
the only individual
who is responsible
for whatever happiness or success
you may attain
is
yourself.

#348

Joy is . . .
having discovered through experience
that the uglier the truth to be told,
the truer the friend is
who tells it to you.

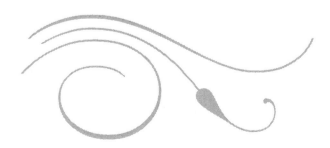

#349

Joy is . . .
when you see
that some of the most edifying
and consequential experiences
you encounter
are completely unexpected, illogical,
random, and spontaneous—
though, oftentimes, perfect.

#350

Joy is . . .
appreciating the fact
that setbacks are really sensational,
because you discover
what doesn't work.

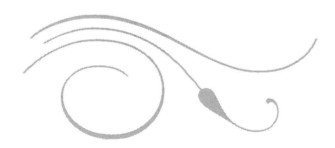

#351

Joy is . . .
when you stop
obsessively thinking about
how stressed you are in your life
and switch to paying attention
to how blessed you are
just to have a life.

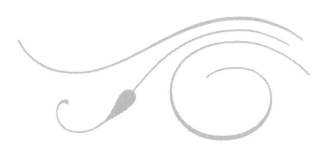

#352

Joy is . . .
daring to take
a single, perilous risk
that completely changes your life
for the better.

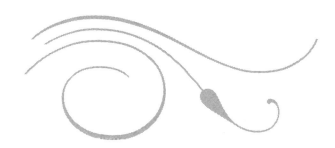

#353

Joy is . . .
being aware that you won't know
how to respect others
if you don't have
self-respect.

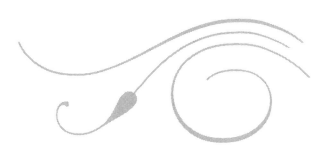

#354

Joy is . . .
believing that
you are defined more
by whom you love
than by what you love.

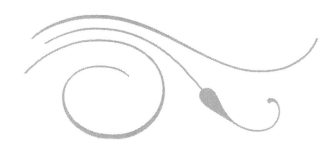

#355

Joy is . . .
whenever you can declutter
your personal ambiance,
not just of useless things,
but of troublesome people,
outmoded ideas,
destructive emotions,
and unwanted habits.

#356

Joy is . . .
what occurs
when you stop making
comparisons.

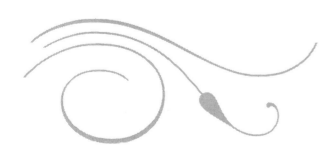

#357

Joy is . . .
understanding that
a focused will to become
is the pivot point
between anger and actualization.

#358

Joy is . . .
when you have the sophistication
to not assume that
personal suffering is inevitable,
because that dreaded state of being
is merely the result of succumbing to
selfish cravings that result in
desire-based actions;
one can change those actions
and escape the associated suffering
by earnestly walking
a more conscious path.

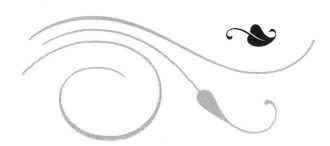

#359

Joy is . . .
living each day
with no particular concern about
how others view you
and with the majority of your attention
focused on how well you know yourself.

#360

Joy is . . .
striving to become
the poster child
for the "Golden Rule."

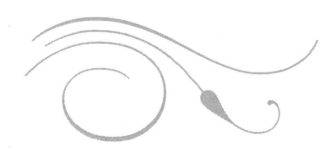

#361

Joy is . . .
setting the clear intent
to have a distinguished existence
and then transforming that intent
into action.

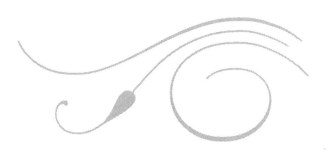

#362

Joy is . . .
bearing in mind
whenever the weight of the world
is upon your shoulders,
that diamonds are just lumps of coal
which have been exposed
to extreme pressure over time.

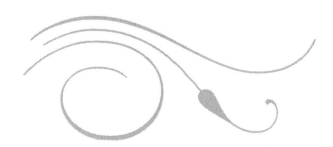

#363

Joy is . . .
what naturally occurs
when you are a valued member
of a purposeful community
filled with active, loving people.

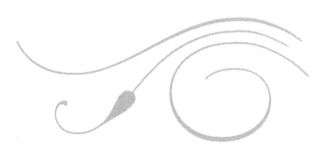

#364

Joy is . . .
the notable awareness
that you are living life well,
when you repeatedly experience
tremendous elation!

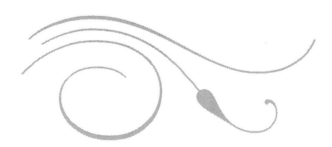

#365

Joy is . . .
the wonderful sense of peace
that pervades your consciousness
whenever you are blessed enough
to discover that,
at the end,
there really is no ending at all;
some other mystery always awaits.

Biography

Paul Abell, Ph.D., could best be described as a modern day renaissance man. He has enjoyed careers in the world of scientific research, psychology, spirituality, art, music, and most notably in the holistic healthcare profession, specializing in integrating Western Psychology with Asian medicine. Since his days as an alternative therapist working with the medical group at the Pritikin Longevity Center in Santa Monica, CA, during the 1980's, he has had an avid interest in the field of longevity. But when he became a father at age 65, his interest in what makes someone live longer turned into a passion for discovering the significant factors common to the "oldest of the old." This book is a summary of some of the more significant keys to living longer that he has discovered over a lifetime of learning.

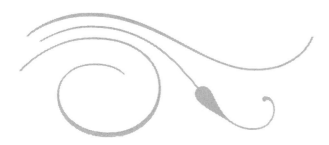

To Contact Dr. Paul Abell

Email: joy.is.book@gmail.com

Facebook: http://facebook.com/Joy is 365 Keys to Longevity

Mailing Address: P. O. Box 2533, Lake Arrowhead, CA 92352

Phone number: 310-922-2245

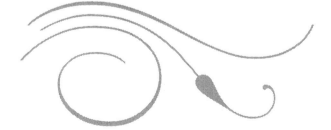

Made in the USA
Middletown, DE
02 February 2019